Much of our nation's early history is shrouded in mystery and one of the most interesting chapters concerns the "cliff dwellers" of America.

Although the cliff dwellers showed great skill in building multiple-story structures, attack-proof villages and practical air-conditioning systems for their underground kivas, they could not overcome drought and famine. Eventually they were forced to abandon their villages but exactly where they went and what happened to them after they left is still not known.

In this book you will find exceptionally fine photographs of their remarkable dwellings and learn much about their cultures and daily life. Such names as Canyon de Chelly, Hovenweep, Wupatki, Bandelier, Mesa Verde and Tonto will take on new and fascinating meaning.

Official maps and descriptions show you where these ruins and restorations are. Perhaps you will be inspired to visit these mysterious "castles" hung amid the high cliffs of our great Southwest.

Writer, illustrator and outdoorsman, C. B. Colby speaks from wide personal experience whether writing about weapons, aviation or the outdoors. His articles have appeared in over twenty-five national magazines, and his more than sixty books have covered almost as many subjects.

During World War II he served as a war correspondent and has traveled from Labrador to Mexico and from Alaska and Hudson Bay to the Caribbean for material for his writings and books.

He is a long time member of the Adventurers Club of New York, the Outdoor Writers Association of America, The American Ordnance Association, and was one of the founders of the Aviation/Space Writers Association. He has been an active member of Civil Air Patrol for over twenty years and holds the rank of Lieutenant Colonel.

Since he first learned to fly gliders in 1931 he has flown, or flown in, almost every kind of aircraft from gliders to jets and from bombers to blimps. His hobbies are camping, firearms, hunting and fishing.

Mr. Colby is married, has two grown children, and lives in Briarcliff Manor, New York.

CLIFF DWELLINGS

Ancient Ruins from America's Past

by C. B. COLBY

Coward-McCann, Inc. New York

Contents

Photo Credits: Union Pacific, page 21. All other photographs, including full color cover transparency, courtesy National Park Service, U. S. Department of the Interior. Photographers: Franklin Wallace, Parker Hamilton, Dick Kent, C. A. Burroughs, Natt Dodge, George A. Grant, and Fred E. Mang, Jr.

08 up

 Manufactured in the United States of America

Library of Congress Catalog Card Number: 65-20512

Riddle of the Ruins

Man has always been curious about his past, but his search for information has often ended in mystery, a sort of historic "dead end." The abandoned cliff dwellings and pueblos of our great Southwest mark one of those dead ends.

Throughout this part of our country, particularly in the "Four Corners" area, where Utah, Colorado, New Mexico and Arizona all touch, there are hundreds of these ruined and deserted adobe and masonry villages and dwellings, silent for centuries.

Once they rang with the voices of adults, the shrill chatter of children, the barking of dogs, and the sounds of livestock. Suddenly, centuries ago, silence crept over these villages and fields, and for hundreds of years the rooms, kivas, gaming areas and once-cultivated fields were silent, except for the occasional crash of falling roofs and walls, and the sounds of wildlife.

Now, many of them once more ring with the voices of people, the chatter of youngsters, and the sounds of feet clambering over paths and up and down ladders. Under the skilled guidance of personnel of the National Park Service, you may now visit many of these long-silent ruins.

There is a fascination in these prehistoric dwellings of centuries-old Americans that intrigues both young and old, and which tantalizes you to visit another ruin and yet another. None are exactly alike and all have their own particular personality and attractions.

The National Park System, a program of the National Park Service of the United States Department of the Interior, is "dedicated to conserving the scenic, scientific and historic heritage of the United States for the benefit of its people." This it is doing magnificently, particularly for future generations!

Through this program and its skilled personnel, many of these mysterious prehistoric dwellings have been restored, strengthened, protected and finally opened for public visits. Many of the sites have marked trails, guided tours, lectures, museums and fine tourist accommodations. Some have campgrounds and trailer parks.

Some of the most remote dwellings are difficult to reach except by horseback or hiking, and some may be visited only with an authorized guide. This is as much for the safety of the visitors as to prevent vandalism, for many of the as yet unreinforced walls of such ruins are weak and dangerous to approach. To enter such an unrestored and protected site might be extremely dangerous.

The Author emerging from a Kiva in Mesa Verde

Much has been learned about the people who lived in these homesites from detailed and careful excavations and expert interpretation of what has been found there.

From pottery fragments, and reconstruction of these pieces into complete vessels, we have learned about their artistic development and their religious ceremonies. From knee, elbow and shoulder indentations in what was once wet plaster walls we have learned about their height and build. From the many types of bones found in their fire pits and refuse dumps we have learned what they ate, hunted for or domesticated, and from scraps of cloth, sandals, and woven mats we have learned of their skills with hand and loom. From bits of weapons and tools we have learned of their intelligence, imagination and ingenuity.

I am sure you will find these ruins exciting, but to visit many of them as I have is even more exciting. Such a visit brings you face to face with life as it must have been in America centuries ago and long before white men set foot upon our shores. Do not fail to visit any of these sites that you can, for thanks to the National Park Service, you can now walk back through history, centuries at a stride, to see how prehistoric American man once lived, built his great masonry villages and — vanished.

I would like to acknowledge with sincere thanks the great help I had from many in the collection of material for this book. In particular I must thank Francis X. Kelly, Press Officer of the National Park Service, for his enthusiastic and skillful assistance in locating photographs and other background material. My thanks also to the personnel of the many National Parks and Monuments involved, for their fine cooperation through Mr. Kelly. Without such traditionally enthusiastic and efficient National Park Service help, this book never would have been possible.

— C. B. COLBY

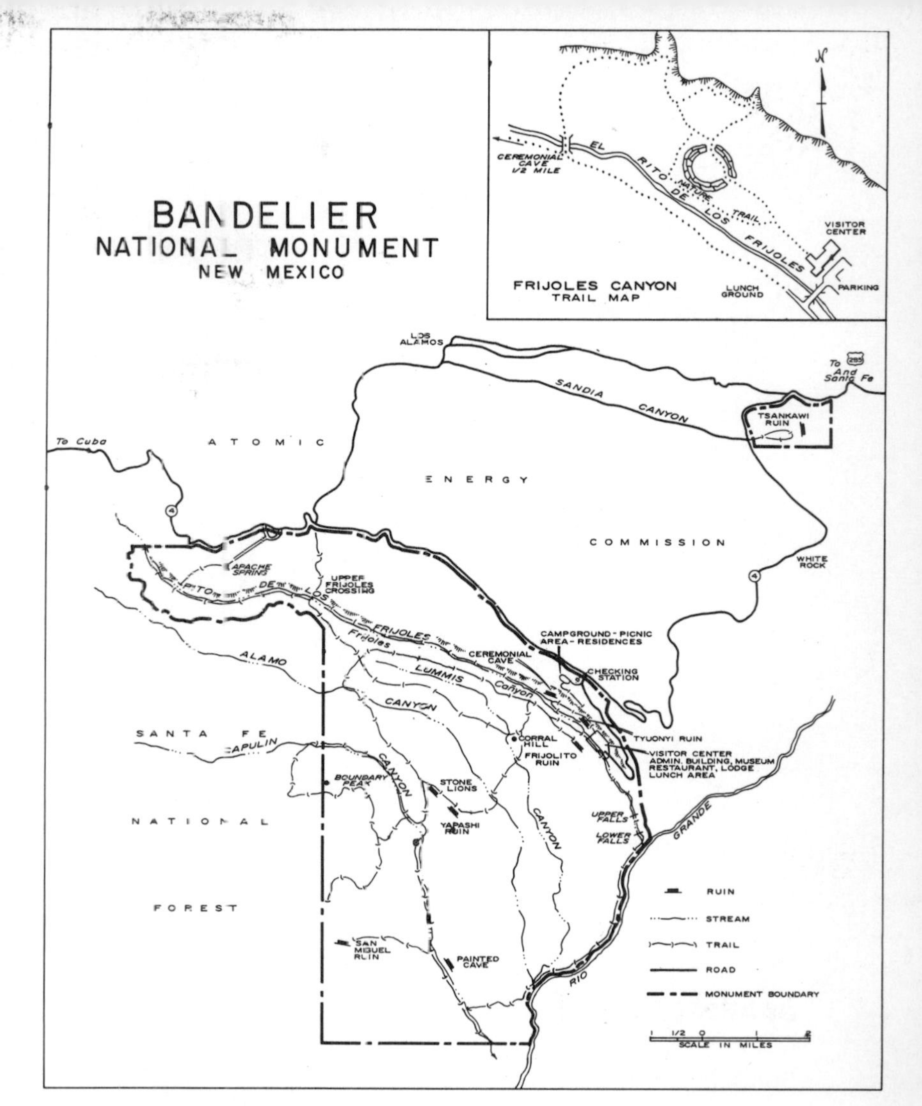

Bandelier National Monument

A little northwest of the center of the state of New Mexico is an unusual area known as the Pajarito Plateau. This is composed almost entirely of "tuff" (consolidated volcanic ash) and basaltic lava thrown out thousands of years ago from the throat of one of the largest — now extinct — volcano craters in the world. Across this great crater floor waters running down to the Rio Grande River have carved steep-walled canyons. It is in the area of these canyons that Bandelier National Monument is located, a 46-square-mile area of wilderness, breathtaking scenery and mysterious dwellings of prehistoric Americans. The map above shows the general plan of the Monument, the roads, trails and ruins. The photo opposite shows some of the Pueblo Indian ruins along the base of one of the cliffs. These are known as "talus villages" and they extend for nearly two miles along these cliff walls. Some of them were as many as three stories high and had rooms carved out of the compressed volcanic ash cliffs behind them. At other points in this area, circular villages were constructed by the inhabitants as early as 1550 A.D. and for some time before; in fact some date as far back as the 12th Century. Many of these people had been driven out of their earlier villages far to the southwest by continued droughts, which sent them straggling north to find water. This they found on the plateau.

Bandelier (continued)

Bandelier National Monument was named in honor of Adolph F. A. Bandelier, a Swiss-American scholar who carried out extensive exploration and survey of the ruins in the region and between 1880 and 1886 studied the Pueblo Indians. The site for the dwellings was well chosen by the builders because it is close to a fine stream, which is almost the only one in the whole area. Its name is quite romantic sounding — "Rito de los Frijoles" — which means simply "Bean Creek" when translated. The masonry ruins have produced many items of pottery and clues to the lives of the builders. They were farmers, growing corn, beans, and squash. They made and used cotton cloth, fragments of which have been found in some of the caves. They also made some pottery which they decorated in glaze with primitive designs. No one knows exactly why the Indians left the area or when. It was perhaps a combination of droughts, flash floods, soil depletion, raiding members of other tribes, or disease. Unquestionably some of the descendants of these early Frijoles inhabitants still live in the modern pueblos along the banks of the Rio Grande.

Bandelier National Monument, 46 miles west of Santa Fe, is reached by U.S. 285 to Pojoaque, then west on Route 4. It is open all year, and overnight accommodations, gasoline and campers' supplies can be obtained during the summer season. There is a good campground on the mesa above Frijoles Canyon. There are 30 miles of hiking trails, a museum, and many interesting things to see within the area.

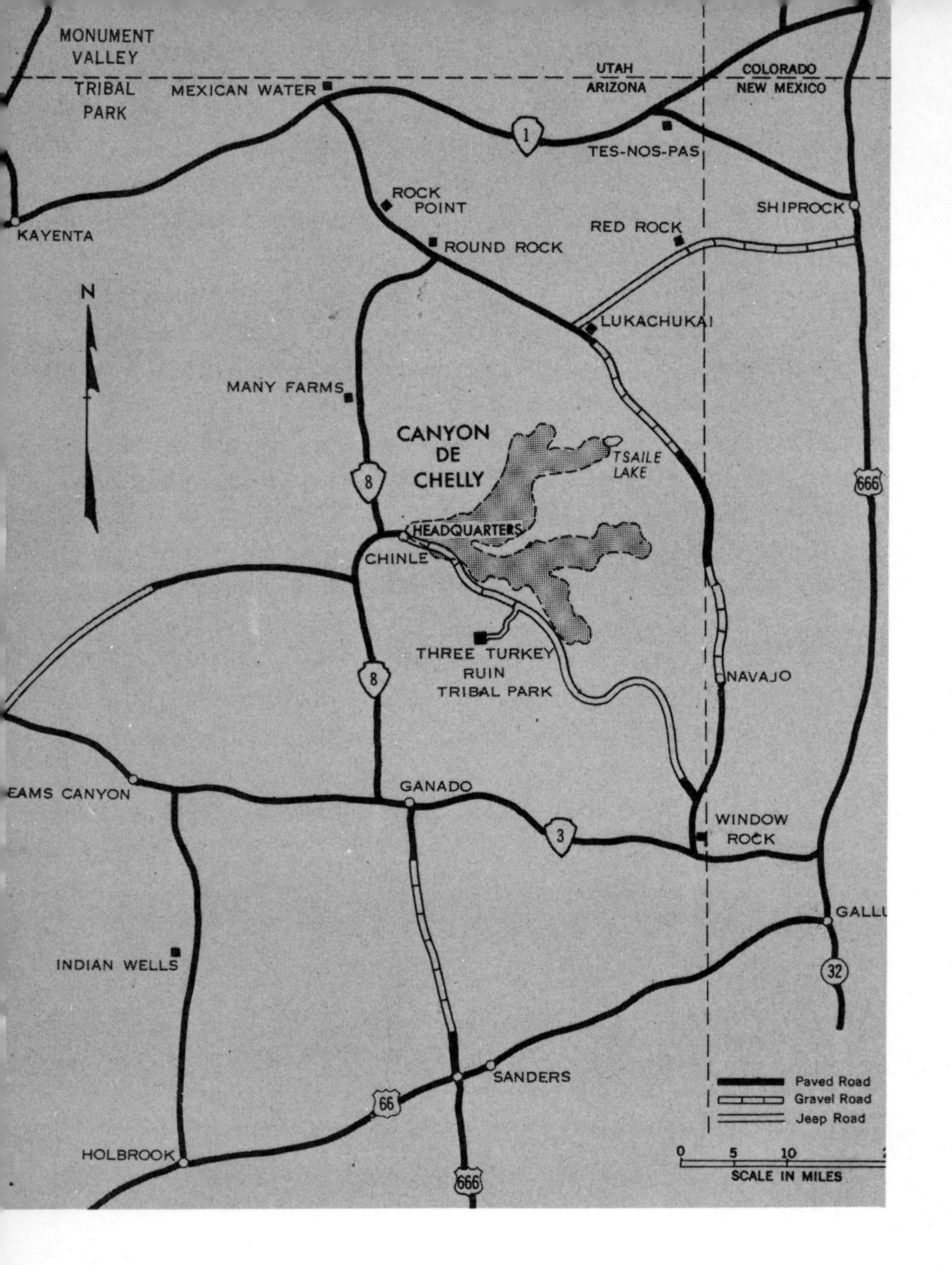

Canyon de Chelly National Monument

Canyon de Chelly (pronounced Canyon de SHAY) is located in the northeast portion of Arizona and was first named in 1882 when an expedition from the famed Smithsonian Institution under James Stevenson found the remains of prehistoric Indian burials in this canyon. The sandstones of this area were laid down over 200 million years ago, and the reddish hues of the vast walls change with the time of day so that they offer a continually changing picture and backdrop for these amazing ruins. In the canyon of the Rio de Chelly there are several hundred prehistoric Indian villages, most of them dating back to between 350 A.D. and 1300 A.D.

The Indians who lived in these villages centuries ago did not use bows and arrows, but spears thrown with the aid of a device called an "atlatl." They grew crops of maize, and squash, and although they did not make pottery, they did make beautiful baskets, sandals and other woven articles. They were known as the Basketmakers. Centuries later they began to make pottery, use bows and arrows and also started to cultivate beans and other vegetables. Their houses changed with the times as well, and instead of the early pit houses — walled structures built over pits in the ground — they became masonry structures as shown in these photos. These were called "pueblos" (Spanish for village). During the 1200's a prolonged drought struck this whole area, with the result that about 1300 the people of the Canyon de Chelly left the area, leaving such splendid examples of their building skills as the so-called Mummy Cave Ruin above.

Canyon de Chelly (continued)

The canyon and its abandoned dwellings were occupied from time to time by other tribes including the Hopi Indians of Arizona who probably lived there during farming season. About 1700, the Navajo Indians, who were concentrated in the northern portions of New Mexico, began to find the canyon attractive and moved in to make it a tribal stronghold. The Navajos raided up and down the Rio Grande Valley until 1864, when a detachment of the United States cavalry headed by Kit Carson finally helped bring the raids to an end. With the removal of about 8,000 of the Navajos to new lands in New Mexico, peace was at least temporarily restored. This first experiment in reservation life was a failure, and four years later the Navajos were permitted to return. Many still live there, farming, raising sheep and serving as guides to the many ruins. Photos above and on opposite page show two views of White House ruins, a most impressive structure still standing in this amazing valley of ruins and the stronghold of the Navajos for many centuries.

This National Monument was established in 1931 and contains more than 130 square miles. You may visit White House Ruin without a guide, but any of the other ruins may be visited only with a Navajo guide or a Park Ranger. This regulation is necessary because there are many dangers in the valley including quicksand, deep dry sand, and flash floods. It is also required that you have a guide along to protect the fragile ruins from damage by vandalism. Many of the ruins and caves contain prehistoric paintings of animals and men, of great historic interest, and they must be protected. The Navajos living in the valley now, live in circular houses made of logs and poles called "hogans." They do some farming but their main industry is raising sheep, a practice they learned from the Spanish back in the 1700's. When you visit this interesting valley remember not to pick up or remove any object, climb or sit on the walls of the ruins, mark or carve anything on ruins or canyon walls, enter an Indian hogan or take photographs of Indians without permission.

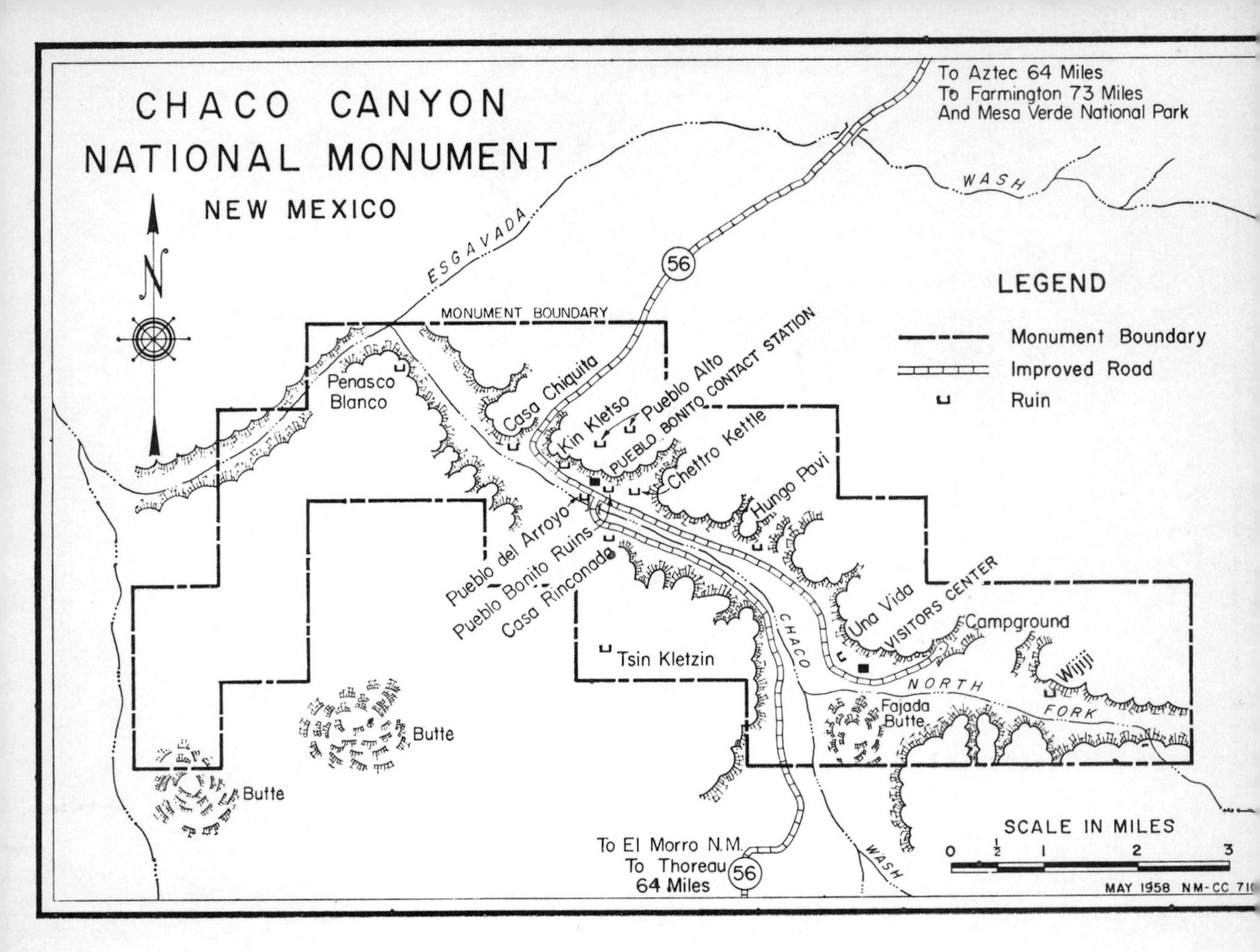

Chaco Canyon National Monument

These well-preserved ruins in New Mexico display the great skill the original builders had in masonry more than a thousand years ago. The great walls and storage buildings, plazas and foundations indicate a high intelligence, natural skill and imagination in architecture. The earliest settlers here were the Basketmaker Indians of an advanced state of cultural development. They knew how to make tools of bone, wood and stone, ornaments and pottery. They progressed so rapidly that by 750 A.D. the end of the Basketmaker period had been reached, and a new one begun, that of the Pueblo culture. With the advent of the new culture, the type of buildings changed from the primitive pit houses to the more imposing masonry structures. The latter rose to several stories and consisted of many rooms.

In this excellent photo of one of the Chaco Canyon ruins you can see the thickness of the building walls, the use of capstones over windows and doors, and the use of heavy timbers to support roofs and floors. There are at least four different methods of laying stone in this building, showing imagination and skill. The row of what look like round windows across the lower portion of the wall in the foreground were where the ends of poles supporting a roof or floor originally rested. In the Chaco Canyon National Monument area there are more than a dozen great ruins similar to this plus over 300 smaller sites where the Indians of that period worked, lived and quarried stone for their buildings. Most of these are within an area about two miles wide and eight miles long.

Chaco Canyon (continued)

This view looking down on the remains of a huge structure shows the many kivas which were built into the ground. Kivas were used by the men of the tribe for clubhouses, clan meetings and ceremonies. One of the ruins, Pueblo Bonito, a huge ruin covering three acres and built to a height of five stories, contained 32 of these men's clubrooms or kivas. These kivas were never used as living quarters and are believed to have originated from the primitive pit houses built by earlier tribes of Basketmakers. In excavating these kivas, great numbers of beautiful ceremonial objects have been discovered, including ornaments of jet and shell, necklaces of turquoise beads, and wooden ornamental plaques. Much trading was done among highly developed tribes, and local minerals were traded for cotton, copper and other items not found locally.

Above is a photo of the Great Kiva found in Casa Rinconada. It is 64 feet in diameter and beautifully constructed. Note the doorway and steps leading into this vast room, the huge base holes for the big posts supporting the roof, and the big fire pit. The circular seat around the walls and the smoothness of the masonry testify to the highly developed skill of these prehistoric masons. The life of these Indians was full of ceremony, trading, and well-developed skills. They domesticated dogs, turkeys and macaws, probably raising the birds for their feathers for ceremonial robes rather than for food alone. The Chacoans farmed and practiced irrigation to help keep crops flourishing. When these intelligent and skillful Indians came here and when they departed is a mystery, but they have left much behind them to be admired and studied for more centuries to come.

Gila Cliff Dwellings National Monument

This small but very interesting cliff dwelling area is located on a small tributary of the west fork of the Gila River, about fifty miles north of Silver City, New Mexico. It is in Gila National Forest and adjacent to the Gila Wilderness Area. The roads into this area are not improved and may be impassable at times, but once you get there the ruins are most interesting indeed. There are six natural caves, all containing ruins, totaling 35 rooms in all. The wood seen at various places in the ruins is original, and helped to date the structures about 1100 A.D. For some unknown reason these structures were abandoned 200 years later (about 1350) and have been vacant ever since except for small animals. The original inhabitants were agriculturists, raising corn, beans, and squash, as well as hunting turkey, deer, elk, and smaller game for food. They were expert potters, making handsome black and white pots, urns and other vessels with great skill. Photo above shows typical Gila Cliff dwelling set well back into a protecting natural cave.

This close-up shows some of the expert masonry found in these structures tucked away in the wind- and erosion-carved cliff caves. These ruins were first discovered in the 1870's by hunters and prospectors who removed many interesting artifacts from them, including arrow shafts, sandals, baskets and pottery. It was made a National Monument in 1907 and contains 533 acres, made up of wild country, cliffs and valleys. There is a small, clear, spring-fed stream which flows along the canyon trail and is believed to be the stream from which the prehistoric builders obtained their water. A half-mile footpath from a parking area at the end of the road brings you to the first of the dwellings. The cliffs are composed of what is called Gila conglomerate, a fairly "crumbly" type of stone which can be worked quite easily. If you visit these primitive ruins you will find no supplies, food or lodgings nearby, although there are places to camp or picnic in the National Forest in which the area is located.

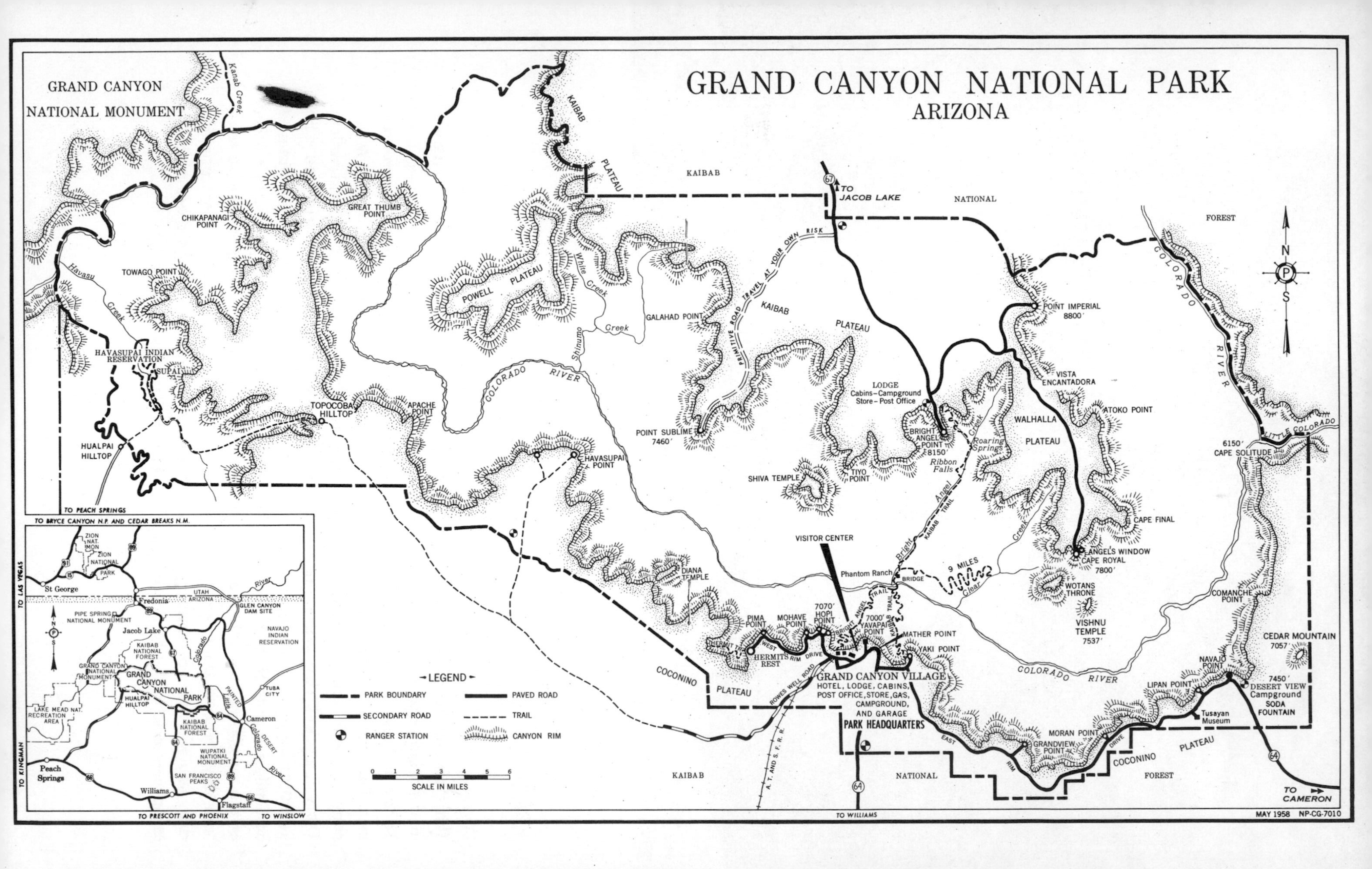
GRAND CANYON NATIONAL PARK
ARIZONA
GRAND CANYON
NATIONAL MONUMENT
Kanab Creek
KAIBAB
PLATEAU
KAIBAB
NATIONAL
FOREST
TO JACOB LAKE
67
CHIKAPANAGI POINT
GREAT THUMB POINT
TOWAGO POINT
POWELL PLATEAU
White Creek
Shinumo Creek
GALAHAD POINT
PRIMITIVE ROAD TRAVEL AT YOUR OWN RISK
KAIBAB
PLATEAU
Havasu Creek
HAVASUPAI INDIAN RESERVATION
SUPAI
TOPOCOBA HILLTOP
APACHE POINT
COLORADO RIVER
HUALPAI HILLTOP
HAVASUPAI POINT
POINT SUBLIME 7460'
SHIVA TEMPLE
TIYO POINT
LODGE
Cabins–Campground
Store–Post Office
BRIGHT ANGEL POINT 8150'
Ribbon Falls
Roaring Springs
Bright Angel Creek
KAIBAB TRAIL
WALHALLA PLATEAU
POINT IMPERIAL 8800'
VISTA ENCANTADORA
ATOKO POINT
CAPE FINAL
ANGEL'S WINDOW
CAPE ROYAL 7800'
WOTANS THRONE
VISHNU TEMPLE 7537'
Clear Creek
9 MILES
6150' CAPE SOLITUDE
LITTLE COLORADO
COMANCHE POINT
CEDAR MOUNTAIN 7057'
TO PEACH SPRINGS
VISITOR CENTER
Phantom Ranch
BRIDGE
DIANA TEMPLE
PIMA POINT
MOHAVE POINT
7070' HOPI POINT
7000' YAVAPAI POINT
MATHER POINT
YAKI POINT
HERMIT TRAIL
HERMITS REST
WEST RIM DRIVE
BRIGHT ANGEL TRAIL
KAIBAB TRAIL
GRAND CANYON VILLAGE
HOTEL, LODGE, CABINS, POST OFFICE, STORE, GAS, CAMPGROUND, AND GARAGE
PARK HEADQUARTERS
ROWES WELL ROAD
A. T. AND S. F. R. R.
COCONINO
PLATEAU
NAVAJO POINT
LIPAN POINT
7450' DESERT VIEW Campground SODA FOUNTAIN
Tusayan Museum
MORAN POINT
GRANDVIEW POINT
EAST RIM DRIVE
COCONINO
PLATEAU
KAIBAB
NATIONAL
FOREST
64
TO CAMERON
TO WILLIAMS
LEGEND
PARK BOUNDARY
PAVED ROAD
SECONDARY ROAD
TRAIL
RANGER STATION
CANYON RIM
0 1 2 3 4 5 6
SCALE IN MILES
MAY 1958 NP-CG-7010
TO BRYCE CANYON N.P. AND CEDAR BREAKS N.M.
TO LAS VEGAS
ZION NAT. MON.
ZION NATIONAL PARK
St George
Fredonia
UTAH
ARIZONA
River
GLEN CANYON DAM SITE
PIPE SPRING NATIONAL MONUMENT
Jacob Lake
NAVAJO INDIAN RESERVATION
KAIBAB NATIONAL FOREST
GRAND CANYON NATIONAL MONUMENT
GRAND CANYON NATIONAL PARK
Colorado
PAINTED DESERT
Little Colorado
TUBA CITY
LAKE MEAD NAT. RECREATION AREA
HUALPAI HILLTOP
Cameron
WUPATKI NATIONAL MONUMENT
SAN FRANCISCO PEAKS
Peach Springs
Williams
Flagstaff
TO KINGMAN
TO PRESCOTT AND PHOENIX
TO WINSLOW

Grand Canyon National Park

Anyone who has stood on the rim of the Grand Canyon in Arizona can easily imagine that there are many cliff dwelling ruins tucked away among its many miles of cliffs, and he is right. More than 600 of these mysterious stone ruins have been discovered so far, and undoubtedly there are many more as yet undiscovered. Some of these, in fact many of them, are almost impossible to reach without special equipment since they are in extremely precipitous places on the faces of vertical cliffs. Some may be completely isolated forever, due to erosion of trails and natural approaches. Some are built high on the canyon walls near the top of the plateaus in small family-sized structures built like stone fortresses. Others are deep in the canyon tucked under overhanging ledges where they were undiscovered for centuries. Photo at the top shows one of the ruins of such a family "fort" made from broken blocks of the native stone upon which it is built. Map on opposite page gives a fine idea of the general canyon area and shows the location of Tusayan Museum (lower right corner of map).

Grand Canyon National Park (continued)

Near the Tusayan Museum is the famous Tusayan Ruin, a stone Indian dwelling built about 1185 A.D. and open to the public. It is one of the few such dwellings that can be reached easily. "Tusayan" is the Spanish name for "Hopi Country." Many of the pueblos and cliff dwellings were discovered in the early days of western exploration and some within recent years, but long before the white man came to the Canyon area they had been abandoned — perhaps centuries before. Probably drought combined with raids by marauding enemies and dwindling game herds forced the inhabitants to leave for other parts of the Southwest. Many of them apparently had small gardens, for traces of them have been found, along with pottery fragments, fragile pieces of cloth and scraps of sandals, and other traces of a long-lost civilization. The Tusayan Museum contains many of these artifacts collected over the years from many of these sites. Photo on opposite page shows one of the isolated cliff dwellings near Moran Point on the South Rim of the Canyon (see map, page 18) on the road from Grand Canyon Village to Tusayan Museum. Note the single ruin below the row of rooms. This may have been a food cache or storage room. Another tiny food cache, tucked under a small overhanging lip of ledge, can be seen about halfway up the left-hand side of the photo. Most of these dwellings had a well-protected approach trail often designed so that a small group of defenders could stand off a whole attacking party with ease, while the rest of the residents escaped by another secret trail. A visit to the Grand Canyon area will be long remembered because of the breathtaking views, fantastic colors and the never to be forgotten feeling of nature's power and grandeur in carving this stupendous natural wonder. It is small wonder that even primitive man and his family wanted to build along its rim and cliffs.

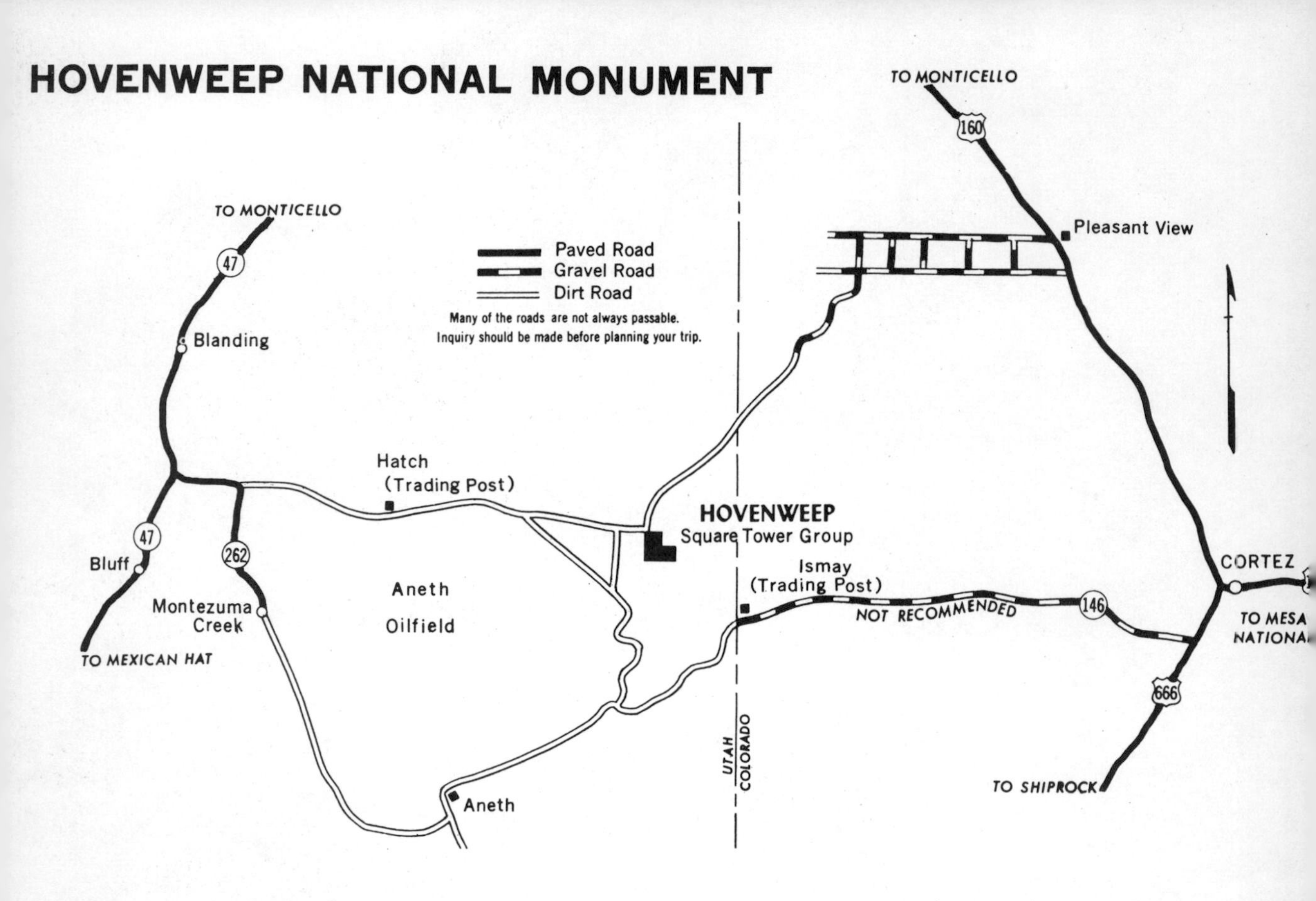

Hovenweep National Monument

Straddling the Utah-Colorado boundary, the Hovenweep National Monument contains some very interesting stone structures erected by prehistoric Indians many centuries ago. These are erected along the very edges of rocky canyons in the famous "Four Corners" region of the Southwest. The people who built these unique structures lived in the area from about 400 to 1300 A.D. and were part of a whole Pueblo civilization. Their culture was identical to that of those living in the Mesa Verde area you will read about later on, and the descendants of these prehistoric people are the present-day Pueblo Indians of New Mexico and Arizona. There are six impressive groups of these stone buildings and towers within the National Monument, plus many small stone "sentry boxes" tucked away in canyon mouths. The main groups include square towers, round towers and some unique "D"-shaped towers with one straight wall and a semicircular wall. Note in photo on opposite page, one of the "D" towers. Some of these ruins consist of a single huge tower, some of twin towers and some of combinations of towers and rooms. All are well designed and exhibit expert masonry. The fact that they have already stood for centuries proves the skill of the builders.

This interesting photo is of Cutthroat Castle, one of the main groups of ruins to be found in the area. The people who lived in the buildings were farmers and when they first came here they lived in caves. Later they began to build these great stone towers and dwellings. They raised corn, beans, squash and cotton in small fields close by. In addition to their crops they used wild plants and hunted wild game and birds for food. They trapped wildlife and domesticated the wild turkey for food and feathers. There were many artists and fine craftsmen among these people, who produced tools, utensils, jewelry, and articles of dress. They also apparently had a well-organized social and religious life which was highly complex. By the early 1100's many outsiders had drifted into the same area and forced many of the Pueblos to move out of their smaller villages. They became concentrated in the larger and more easily defended villages near the heads of the canyons, which had permanent springs of water. Here they could defend their water supply along with their stock and families. In about 1276 a twenty-three year drought began which resulted in the complete abandonment of the valley about 1300 or some time before then, with the people never returning. The name "Hovenweep" is the Ute Indian word for "deserted valley" and seems most suitable for this wild and mysterious area dotted with silent ruins and peopled with the spirits of the long vanished race that built them.

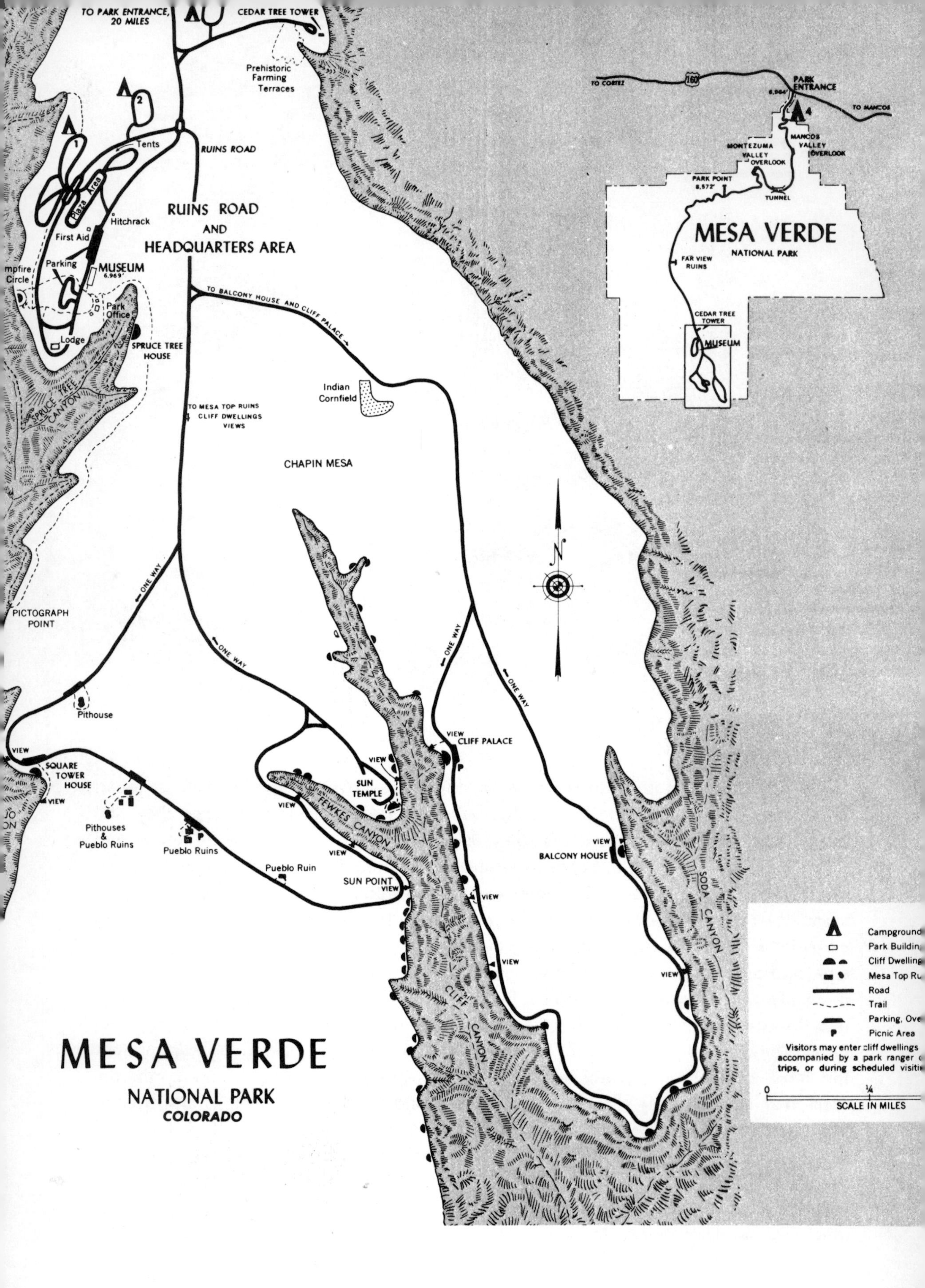

TO PARK ENTRANCE, 20 MILES
CEDAR TREE TOWER
Prehistoric Farming Terraces
2
1
Tents
RUINS ROAD
Plaza Area
Hitchrack
RUINS ROAD AND HEADQUARTERS AREA
First Aid
Parking
MUSEUM 6,969'
Campfire Circle
Park Office
Lodge
SPRUCE TREE HOUSE
SPRUCE TREE CANYON
TO BALCONY HOUSE AND CLIFF PALACE
Indian Cornfield
TO MESA TOP RUINS CLIFF DWELLINGS VIEWS
CHAPIN MESA
N
ONE WAY
PICTOGRAPH POINT
ONE WAY
ONE WAY
ONE WAY
Pithouse
VIEW
SQUARE TOWER HOUSE
VIEW
Pithouses & Pueblo Ruins
Pueblo Ruins
Pueblo Ruin
VIEW
SUN TEMPLE
VIEW
FEWKES CANYON
VIEW
SUN POINT VIEW
VIEW
CLIFF PALACE
VIEW
VIEW
CLIFF CANYON
VIEW
BALCONY HOUSE
SODA CANYON
VIEW
MESA VERDE
NATIONAL PARK
COLORADO
TO CORTEZ
160
PARK ENTRANCE
6,964'
TO MANCOS
4
MONTEZUMA VALLEY OVERLOOK
MANCOS VALLEY OVERLOOK
PARK POINT 8,572'
TUNNEL
MESA VERDE
NATIONAL PARK
FAR VIEW RUINS
CEDAR TREE TOWER
MUSEUM
Campground
Park Buildin
Cliff Dwellin
Mesa Top Ru
Road
Trail
Parking, Ove
Picnic Area
Visitors may enter cliff dwellings
accompanied by a park ranger
trips, or during scheduled visit
0
¼
SCALE IN MILES

Mesa Verde National Park

One of the most popular and extensive of all cliff dwelling sites is Mesa Verde ("Green Table") in Colorado. About 1 A.D. wandering Indians came to this area and began to settle down. They were farmers and at first built simple pit houses, which merely consisted of circular shallow pits in the ground with low walls and a simple roof overhead of sticks, brush and hides. Those who settled in the Mesa Verde region did not even have to build these shelters for they could find adequate shelter in the many huge caves in the cliffs. These primitive people were clever weavers of baskets, bags, sandals, mats and other articles. For this reason they were referred to by archaeologists as basket-weavers, or basketmakers. They were actually Pueblo Indians in an early state of cultural development. On the opposite page is a map of the Mesa Verde National Park area atop the "Green Table," and above, a photo of the first of the many dwellings discovered by W. H. Jackson, famous pioneer photographer, in 1874. This is known as the Two Story Cliff House, and at the time of discovery held many fine artifacts which gave numerous clues to the life of these prehistoric Indians.

Mesa Verde (continued)

Above and on opposite page are views of the Cliff Palace Ruins tucked away under a mighty overhanging ledge in one of the canyons. This village once held several hundred Indians of all ages. Note the round and square towers, some several stories high. The round foundations usually indicate kivas or underground club or ceremonial rooms, while the square walls and ruins are typical of dwellings, storage rooms and protective walls. Almost every cliff dwelling village had one or more kivas, indicating a very complex religious system and a culture fond of ceremonies. These underground kivas had complicated and ingenious air-conditioning tunnels and heating pits for fires. In about 450 A.D. the basketmakers began to make pottery, use the bow and arrow and also started construction of the far more substantial houses made of masonry as these are. Some of the earlier settlers here built dwellings on top of the mesas, but as dangers threatened they gradually moved from their fortified mesa top pueblos to the well-protected caves below the rim, where they built these fabulous structures. The author has climbed through many of them and was amazed at the skill and imagination in their design and construction. Many a tiny path to a village could be protected from the ports in a stone tower, where a single archer with a goodly supply of arrows could protect an entire village from attack. Cliff Palace is the largest of Mesa Verde Ruins but not the best preserved.

Mesa Verde (continued)

Above is a wide view of another of these amazing masonry villages under the cliffs of Mesa Verde. The broad flat areas were used for tribal activities and the tiny stone rooms high on the cliff shelves above the main buildings were used as food storage bins. On the opposite page is a close-up of part of this same village to show the thick stone block walls. Imagine the work required for such construction without modern tools, or hoists. In many places the walls are cleverly fitted into the irregular face of the cliff itself to make a tight seal against the weather. Thousands of tons of rock had to be moved and put into place to construct these multi-room and many-storied dwellings. The lives of the inhabitants changed from century to century as new ideas were adopted along with new skills. Pottery became more and more beautiful and the designs more complicated. Pottery vessels were simple — made by coiling ropes of clay and pinching the coils together. There were two main types of vessels — those for storage or cooking, on which the coils were left visible; and those for ceremonial use or eating, which were smoothed and decorated with black designs on a white background. The loom was introduced along with cotton for making articles of clothing. The season on the Mesa was too short to grow cotton so it was probably bartered for, either as fibers or perhaps as cloth itself.

Mesa Verde (continued)

Of the many cave-located cliff dwellings at Mesa Verde, some are tiny stone rooms used for food storage tucked away on almost unreachable cliff shelves. Others are elaborate and complicated and capable of providing shelter for hundreds. Here are three more fine examples of these ruins. This photo shows Square Tower House, while opposite page (top) shows Spruce Tree House and (lower) Balcony House. Find these on the map on page 24. Not all of the ruins shown in this section are shown on map. Unfortunately these great ruins, once built, were not to be occupied for long, for by the end of the 13th Century a 23-year drought combined with other unknown factors triggered a complete mass exodus. Just why these intelligent and talented Indians should have given up all they had built over the centuries and leave for other areas is not known, but before the end of the 12th Century most of these particular villages were deserted, and by the end of the 14th Century even those in other parts of the region had been deserted, leaving the entire "Four Corners" part of the country abandoned by the Pueblos. Left behind were empty rooms, hundreds of artifacts in the shape of pottery, sandals, food, scraps of clothing, mats, tools and a few weapons, all that is left of a once powerful race of cliff dwellers. Visiting Mesa Verde is a thrilling return to the past and many millions visit it each year. Do not fail to visit this amazing collection of ruins if you possibly can.

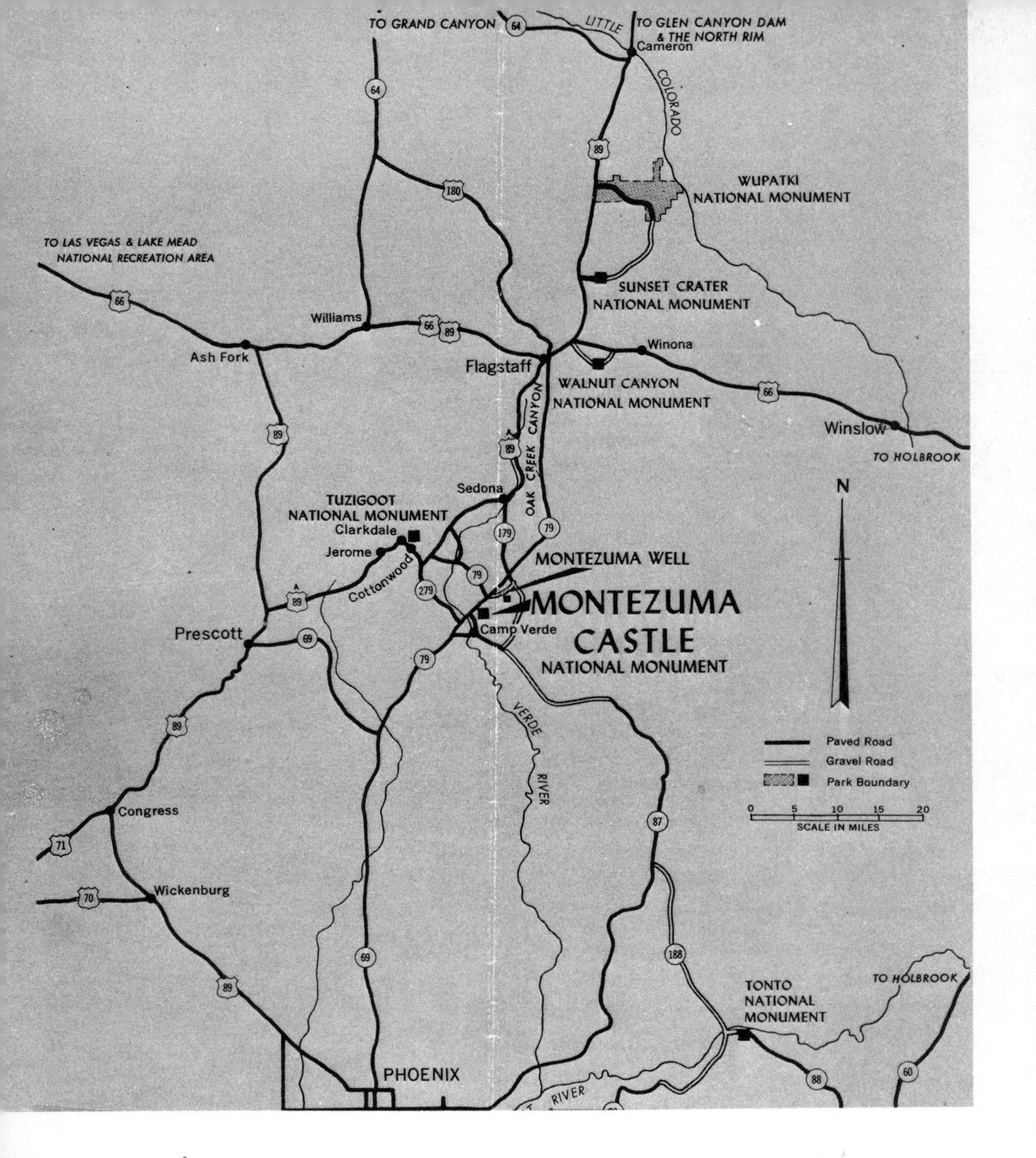

Montezuma Castle National Monument

One of the most interesting and best preserved of all America's cliff dwellings is found in Verde Valley in central Arizona. Along the limestone cliffs of Beaver Creek are several ruins dating back to about 900 A.D. The residents were industrious farmers and at first lived in little pole-and-brush houses. Later, about 1100, others joined them, and by 1250 they were building strong, defensible pueblos both on the hills near their fields and in a few caves. The ruins now found in this National Monument were constructed more recently. Some of these have 45 rooms and are five-story structures that held as many as fifteen families. The map above shows major sites of this area.

This photo shows Montezuma Castle, one of the exciting ruins found in Montezuma Castle National Monument. It is perched high on a cliff above the valley floor and is especially well preserved. This fine pueblo was abandoned by about 1450. It is quite possible that a prehistoric "population explosion" caused the abandonment of these dwellings; just too many people for the food the area could provide. A few miles away can be found what is known as Montezuma Well, a huge limestone sink half filled with water and fed by springs. This natural supply of water flows at the rate of 1,500,000 gallons a day and the Indians built stone irrigation ditches to carry this water to their farmlands in the valley below. There are several smaller cliff dwellings around this huge well but they too were deserted when the food-raising ability of the area was exhausted. These rural Indians were clever at many things but their pottery consisted mainly of plain red or brown ware, almost all undecorated. They did, however, create some exceptionally fine turquoise and shell jewelry, produced stone implements and elaborately decorated cotton cloth.

Montezuma Castle National Monument (continued)

This photo shows one of the lesser ruins in the Monument, but one that is of interest to visitors because of the many small food storage "bins" tucked away in tiny caves in the cliff. The soft stone was once a vast lake bed of lime-filled mud. This old lake drained away perhaps two million years ago leaving the bed exposed. Eventually it eroded away, leaving the cliffs which in turn eroded, forming overhanging ledges and many caves in which the prehistoric Indians built their dwellings and stored their food. Very little is known about some of their culture and only from the artifacts discovered in their pueblo areas were we able to learn what we have. This interesting collection of cliff dwellings was not named after Montezuma, the Aztec emperor, but by early settlers who discovered the ruins and thought they had been built by Aztec refugees fleeing from Mexico during the time of the Spanish conquest. This National Monument was established in December 1906 and contains about 842 acres in two sections.

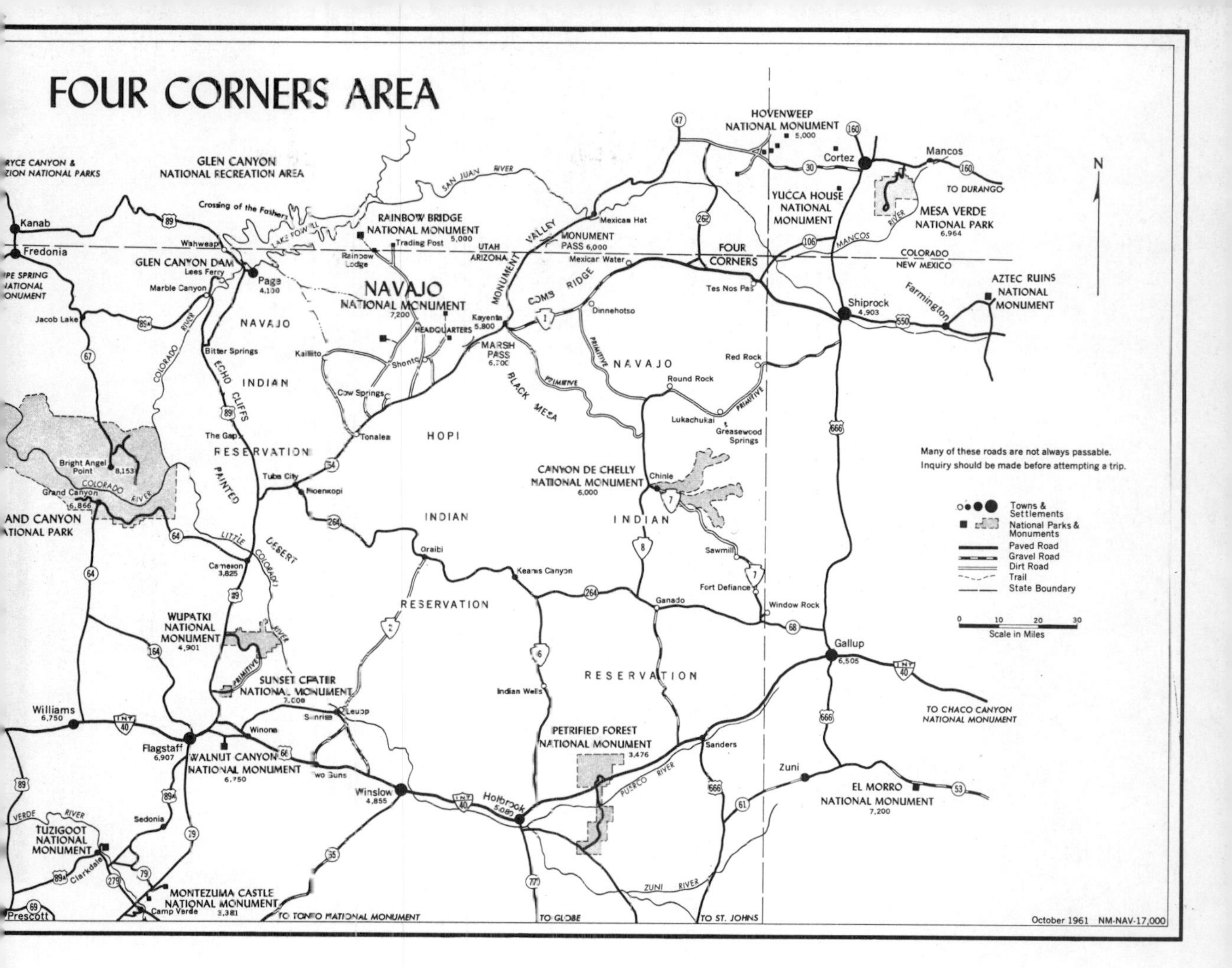

Navajo National Monument

The "Four Corners" area, the only place in the United States where the corners of four states — Colorado, New Mexico, Utah and Arizona — come together and where you can lie on your stomach with an arm or leg in each of four states at the same time (the author has done this silly thing), is full of these prehistoric cliff dwellings. One of the many National Monuments in this area, as you can see from the map above, is the Navajo National Monument, established in March 1909. It consists of an area of 360 acres which is surrounded by the Navajo Indian Reservation and is on the edge of a vast roadless area. There are three cliff dwellings of importance in the Monument which were occupied from about 300 A.D. until about the year 1300 A.D. Those prehistoric Indians are now called "Anasazi," from the Navajo name meaning "ancient ones." Originally nomadic, they finally settled in this area and, as their population increased, they built more and more substantial homes. Their culture developed and then, tragically, it came to a sudden halt and a gradual decline of the entire Indian population of the area began. A combination of circumstances brought about the end of the decline, and end of this interesting civilization.

Navajo National Monument (continued)

Chief among these unfortunate events was perhaps soil erosion, brought about by overplanting in an attempt to keep up with the growing population, drought, and generally poor farming practices. This reduction of food supplies caused many to move away to better farming areas and soon the remaining Anasazi abandoned the great pueblos, leaving them to history and an occasional wandering Indian or inquisitive animal. By about 1350 the ruins were silent. Photo above shows one small portion of the ruin of Betatakin meaning "Hillside House" which once contained almost 150 rooms. There are several cliff paintings in the area. In photo opposite note shield of war god on eastern wall of Betatakin Ruin. In one other ruin a few miles away there is an inscription in Spanish which dates back to 1661. This National Monument was established in March of 1909 and, while rather remote, is well worth a visit. Much of the area requires a guide and trips by horseback (both guides and horses obtainable in Monument) along unmarked trails, but the views and experience are well worth it.

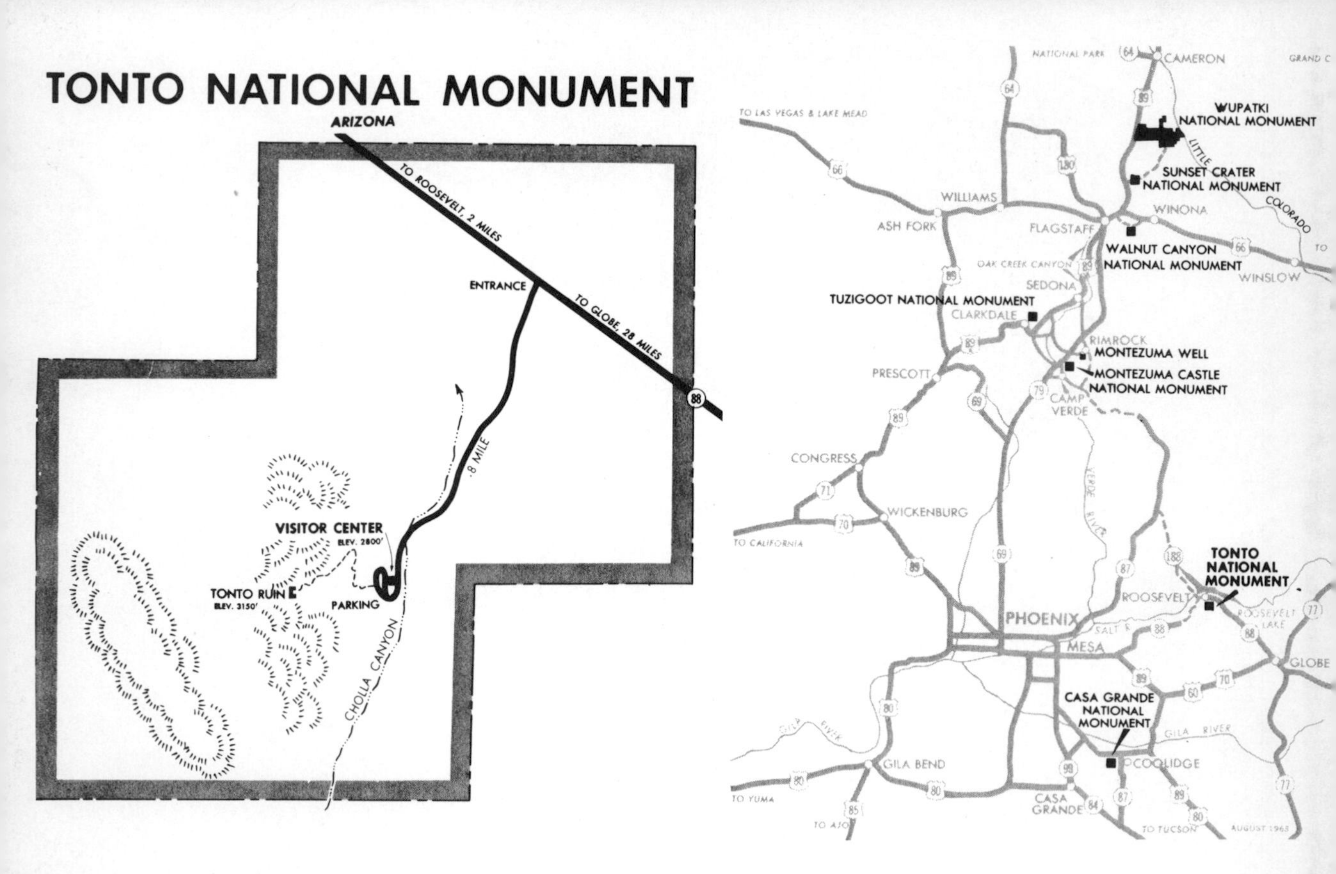

Tonto National Monument

Another group of Arizona's mysterious cliff dwellings can be found in Tonto National Monument, established in December 1907. Here you will find three multi-room cliff dwellings tucked into erosion-carved caves in a mountainside. These were built and occupied during the 1300's by a southern Arizona group of Pueblo Indians, now known as "Salado" Indians. "Salado" is Spanish for "salty" and the name was applied to these cliff dwellers because they lived near the Salt River, as you can see from the map. The Salado Indians were farmers and quite skillful agriculturalists. They used irrigation ditches to bring water from the Salt River to their fields which were located two to four miles from their homes. They raised cotton, pumpkins, beans (several kinds), corn, squash, gourds, and grain amaranth. This is the first evidence that grain amaranth was ever raised as a cultivated crop by man. They used many kinds of wild plant foods, nuts and fruits, as well as wild game for food, in addition to their cultivated crops. Among the animal bones found in the ruins were those of deer, rabbit, pronghorn antelope, gray fox, bobcat, cougar, badger, bighorn sheep, porcupine, prairie dog and also the bones of many birds.

Photo above shows what is called the Lower Ruin of the three in this group at Tonto National Monument. You can see how the buildings, set well back into the natural cave, almost filled it before time and the centuries destroyed much of the masonry. The other two ruins in this group, Lower Ruin Annex and Upper Ruin, are very similar in cave setting and type of buildings. They were made from unshaped native quartzite, laid up with adobe mortar. The walls were built in sections, one stone in thickness and plastered on the inside. The floors also were adobe and the roofs were poles overlaid with smaller poles and topped with a three- or four-inch layer of adobe. Although these people were of prehistoric times they were very intelligent and artistic. They were expert at producing much colored pottery with high-gloss interiors and excellent decorations in red and black. They were also very skilled at weaving, making items of cotton material dyed in many colors. Included in these colors were brown, black, white, yellow, deep blue, dark green and blue-black. The last two colors have not been recorded as found in any other site. They made many fine tools from stone, including arrowheads, hammers, knives and arrowshaft straighteners. From shells they made pendants, bracelets, beads and other personal ornaments. Many of these shells came from the Gulf of Mexico, which indicates a wide trading program with other tribes.

Tonto National Monument (continued)

These intelligent craftsmen also used wood in many ways. They used it in their homes and for making tools, weapons, cradleboards, clubs, looms and games. From cane they made arrows, pipes, and some baskets. They also used beargrass for weaving carrying straps, lines, cradleboard fittings and similar items in common use. From artifacts found in and about these ruins much can be told of what these Indians looked like. More information has been gathered from human remains found in burial sites. The Salados were short but muscular. The women averaged less than five feet tall,. while the men were perhaps a few inches taller. They were slight and had dark skins and dark eyes. Many had very poor teeth because of the bits of stone in the meal, ground in stone mortars with stone pestles (grinding tools). The clothing for women consisted of small cotton blankets worn about the shoulders and a small skirt or apron of yucca cord. The men wore headbands, small blankets, and breechclouts. Both men and women wore sandals for walking on the rocky slopes. From artifacts we know their living quarters were well furnished for the period of culture. They contained a fire pit in the center (usually) with cooking pots and bowls, fire-making equipment (bow drill and baseboards were used) brushes of grass stems, torches of juniper bark for light, weaving and spinning implements and mats for sleeping and sitting. These dwellings were abandoned about 1400 A.D., but no one knows why. Their homes were well built and well protected, their rich well-irrigated fields were still producing and there was plenty of water. Their leaving is just another of the mysteries of our great Southwest and its prehistoric residents.

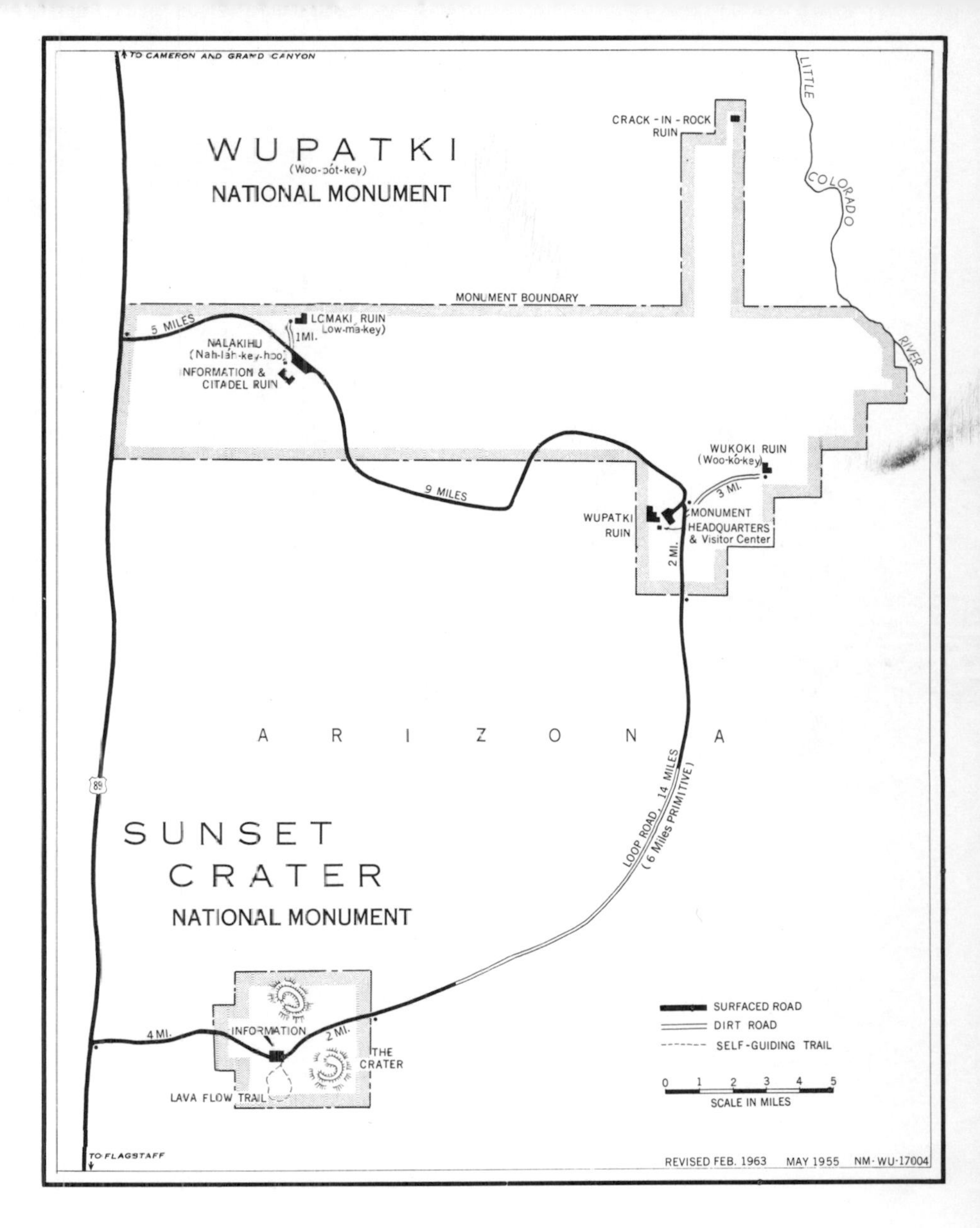

Wupatki National Monument

About 600 A.D. a few prehistoric farming Indians moved into the area near the San Francisco Peaks in Arizona. They lived in pit houses, but only a few could stay because of a lack of moisture and limited farming areas. These few remained for several centuries, barely able to make a living from the poor soil and almost waterless land. In about 1064 A.D. these Indians were startled into panic by a volcanic eruption from what is now Sunset Crater National Monument, about fourteen miles to the southwest. Those living close to the volcano fled in terror as their homes were bombarded with hot rocks and cinders. When the eruptions ended a new cinder cone 1,000 feet high had been formed and for hundreds of miles around, the ground was covered with black volcanic ash. This catastrophe was a blessing in the long run, for the ash enriched the soil so that it became excellent farmland, causing many Indians to return to the area to take up agriculture in a far larger way than ever before.

Wupatki National Monument (continued)

The word about this suddenly fertile land soon spread and Indians flocked into the area from far and near to raise corn where the plants had previously withered and died. The area became the target for a sudden land boom of prehistoric times and a melting pot for Indians of many cultures and backgrounds. Pueblo villages sprang up all over the area and one of the largest and longest inhabited is now known as Wupatki, a Hopi word for "tall house." Located near one of the few springs in the entire area, it grew until it held at least 250 to 300 persons, was at least three stories high, and consisted of more than a hundred rooms. It was built of red sandstone and the walls were wide and strong and held together with adobe. The map shows the location of both the dwellings and the craters to the southwest from which the volcanic ash came. The Wupatki National Monument contains 56 square miles and the Sunset Crater National Monument contains 4½ square miles of Monument land. Photo above shows one section of this huge ruin, showing some of the various levels of construction.

This photo shows a close-up of one portion of the Wupatki Ruins, showing the excellent type of strong construction used to support the heavy rooms and floors. A few yards away from this and other structures a huge circular amphitheater has been excavated, where public ceremonies were held. All in all there are about 800 Indian ruins in the Monument area, some just small earth lodges and some large pueblos of many rooms. Within a single square mile of territory over 100 sites can be found. Many of them are as yet unexcavated. This National Monument was created in December 1924, and is one that will reveal more and more often surprising facts about the prehistoric residents as excavations continue. For example, near the great ruins of Wupatki a playing field or ball court of stone masonry has been found, one of two in the vicinity. Little is known of the game that was played there but at least their lives were not all work and no play. Eventually winds like those which had brought the life-giving ash to the fields began to strip it away again. Soon the fields could no longer produce enough food to support the big population and many people began to drift away. By the 1300's there was no one left and another great pueblo village was left to the winds and weather, due to wind erosion of the soil and the long drought of 1276–99.

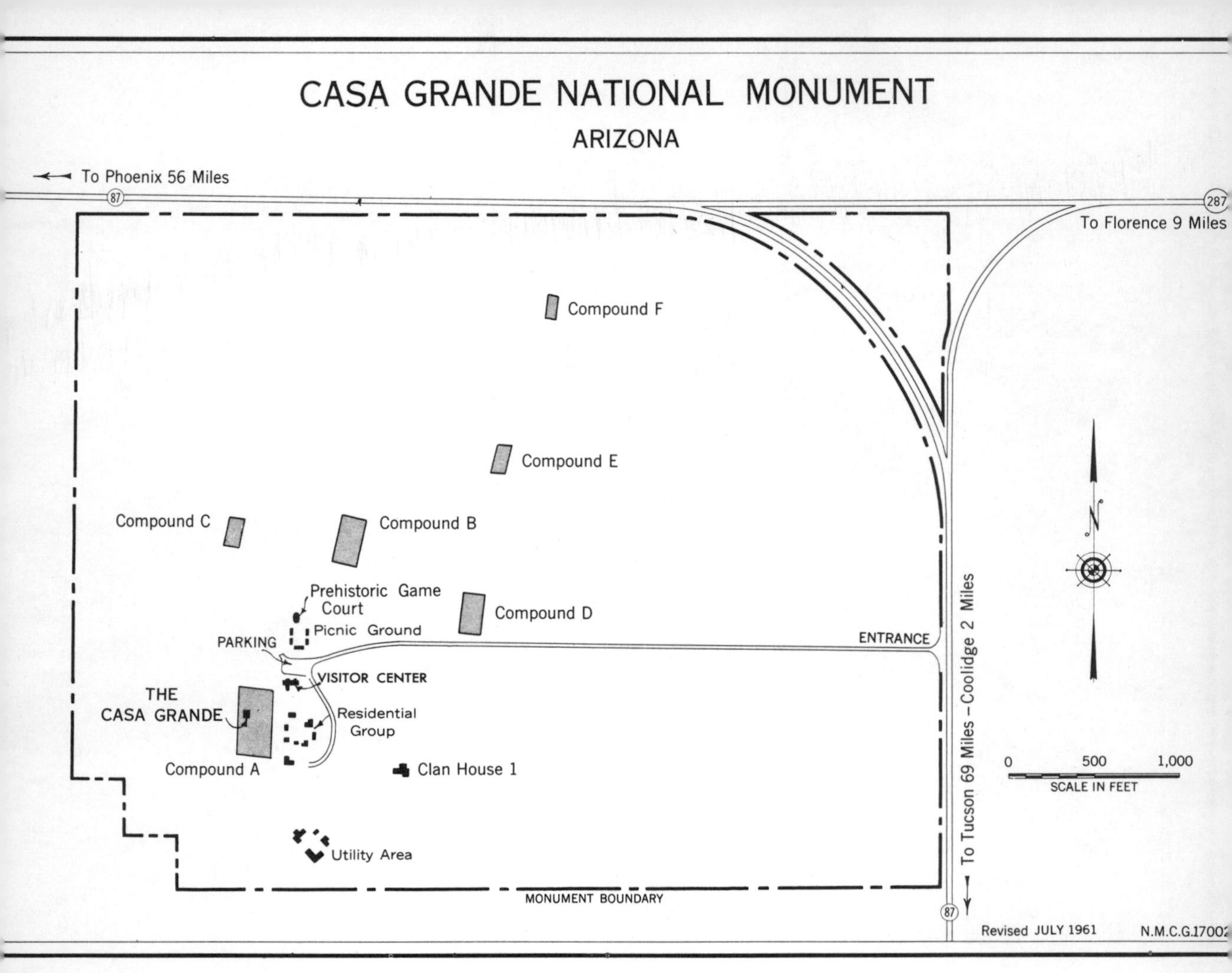

Casa Grande Ruins National Monument

Although this amazing structure is not a cliff dwelling in the true sense, it is so unusual (it is the only surviving example of such a structure) and so closely linked with other pueblo builders including the cliff dwellers, it has a place in this book. Casa Grande Ruins National Monument was established in 1918, although it had been under Congressional protection since 1889 when the lands nearby, including these ruins, were reserved by the President. The Monument now includes 475 acres and much excavation is still being carried out. The map above shows the general layout and location of this very important National Monument. The first Indians began to farm this part of Arizona at about the beginning of the Christian era, and used small-scale irrigation ditches to bring water to their fields. These early residents were called (by modern residents) the "Hohokams," meaning "The Ancient Ones" in the language of the Pima Indians. They lived in simple single-room homes of brush and mud. Their crops were maize, beans, pumpkins, and cotton. Their dead were cremated and they were very proficient in carving stone and shells. They made both cooking and ceremonial vessels of pottery, buff in color and often decorated with red paint.

By the year 700 these "ancient ones" had launched a dramatic irrigation ditch building program. They constructed these vast ditches by hand to a width of 25 feet and a depth, in places, of 15 feet. Over the following years these were extended so that some of them reached a length of 22 miles! During the centuries many tribes moved into the area, mingling with the Hohokams and exchanging ideas and cultures. Gradually the Puebloan culture dominated that of the Hohokams and even their buildings assumed the appearance of the pueblos from other areas: many roomed structures, and often walled against attacks from a possible enemy. In some areas high thick-walled watchtowers were built. The Casa Grande shown in the photo above is the lone remaining example of these uniquely constructed structures. This building was made from a material called "caliche" found several feet below the desert surface. It was a clay with a high content of lime. This building was four stories high and was built on stout foundations sunk thirty inches into the ground. The walls were built in layers — when one layer was hard, another layer was built on top of it. When the walls were seven feet high the enclosure was filled with dirt. This formed the first story and two additional stories were built on top of it. On top of the third story a small central room was built, forming the fourth story. What this type of construction amounted to was an artificial seven-foot hill with a three-story house on top of it. Besides serving as a watchtower the building had eleven living rooms. It was probably built during the 1300's and used for a few generations only, for by 1450 it had been abandoned.

Casa Grande Ruins National Monument (continued)

As the people drifted away leaving behind their many pueblos, wind and weather soon began to destroy them. The great ruins of Casa Grande also soon began to crack and crumble. In 1932 the cement and steel shelter shown on pages 45 and 48 was erected over this unique ruin to protect it from the drying sun and rains. In the ruins of this and other surrounding pueblo ruins many artifacts were found (above), and on opposite page are shown some of them. At the top of this page are examples of fine black and white pottery. Below this are examples of earlier pottery, either plain buff or red and buff. On the opposite page are fine examples of rings, bracelets, stone and pottery sculpture and even a bone whistle. Note the interesting face at upper right and the quite modern-looking bird just above the plaque. Through the skill of archaeologists many of these have been restored from small and scattered pieces, often picked up over a wide area and painstakingly fitted together like a difficult jigsaw puzzle — an intriguing phase of a fascinating profession which may be worth investigating as a possible career.

This close-up of the shelter and ruins of Casa Grande shows to what lengths the National Park Service of the Department of Interior has gone to help preserve this unique prehistoric ruin for future generations. When you visit some of these cliff dwellings, as I know you will, keep in mind that many more generations after you will want to see them as they are. Do not remove or deface any wall or structure. Do not remove or displace any stones, artifacts you might see, or signs put there for your guidance. Enjoy them as they are, as they have been for centuries, and leave them as they are for other people in the centuries to come.